Recipes for a
MEDIEVAL
FEAST

Working Flexibly with Fractions

Janey Levy

PowerMath™

The Rosen Publishing Group's

PowerKids Press™
New York

The recipes in this book are intended for a student to make together with an adult.

Published in 2007 by The Rosen Publishing Group, Inc.
29 East 21st Street, New York, NY 10010

Book Design: Michael Tsanis

Photo Credits: Cover, p. 8 © Archivo Iconografico, S.A./Corbis; p. 4 © Jim Zuckerman/Corbis; p. 7 © Francis
G. Mayer/Corbis; pp. 10, 30 © Bettman/Corbis; pp. 11, 12, 15, 16, 18, 27 (cinnamon) by Michael Tsanis;
p. 14 © Lee Snider/Photo Images/Corbis; p. 19 © Paul Poplis/FoodPix; p. 20 © Michael Freeman/Corbis;
pp. 21, 23, 25, 28 by Janey Levy; p. 24 © Gianni Dagli Orti/Corbis; p. 26 © PhotoDisc; p. 27 (nutmeg) ©
Wolfgang Kaehler/Corbis; p. 29 © John Heseltine/Corbis.

Library of Congress Cataloging-in-Publication Data

Levy, Janey.
  Recipes for a medieval feast : working flexibly with fractions / Janey Levy.
      p. cm. — (Math for the real world)
  Includes index.
  ISBN 1-4042-3354-7 (lib. bdg.)
  ISBN 1-4042-6061-7 (pbk.)
  ISBN 1-4042-6062-5 (6 pack)
  1. Fractions—Juvenile literature. 2. Arithmetic—Juvenile literature. 3. Cookery, Medieval—History—
Juvenile literature. I. Title. II. Series.

QA117.L62 2006
513.2'6—dc22

                                                          2005014306

Manufactured in the United States of America

Contents

What Was the Medieval Period?

The medieval period was an era of European history that lasted from about A.D. 400 to about A.D. 1400. "Medieval" is a Latin word that means "having to do with the Middle Ages." The Middle Ages got their name from **Renaissance** scholars, who saw the period simply as a middle time between the fall of the Roman Empire in the 400s and the rebirth of classical learning during the Renaissance of the 1400s. The name suggests that this was a period when interesting or important events did not happen. However, that is not true.

People of the Middle Ages enjoyed a rich, vibrant culture. Music was composed. Beautiful artworks were created. The great cathedrals of Europe were built during this time. Large cities grew up across Europe. Banking and commerce became important parts of the economy. Europeans set out to explore the world beyond their borders.

In this book, we're going to get a taste of the Middle Ages—literally. We're going to learn about the Middle Ages through the era's food. To do that, we're going to need math skills, since preparing food requires math. We especially need to be able to work with fractions. However, before we get to the recipes, let's learn a little more about life during the medieval period.

Bruges, Belgium, still looks much like it did in the Middle Ages. Linked to the North Sea by a canal, the city was an important commercial and banking center during the Middle Ages. Merchants from all over Europe settled here to conduct trade. Luxury items from around the world, like costly spices, passed through the city.

Medieval Society

Medieval society was **feudal**. At the top of medieval society was the king, who ruled a large territory. Below the king were lords. Each lord governed his own territory, but he pledged to obey, support, and—if necessary—fight for the king. At the bottom were the serfs, or peasants. They worked the land for the lords. Serfs kept part of what they raised and gave the rest to their lord. In return, the lord provided protection for the serfs.

Life differed greatly between the top and bottom of medieval society. Kings and lords had 1 or more large castles in which to live. Beautiful objects filled the castles, and kings, lords, and their families wore expensive clothes and jewels. Serfs lived in small houses and had few possessions.

Foods also differed greatly. The serfs' diet centered around dark, heavy bread made from rye or barley and a thick soup called pottage (PAH-tihj). Onions, cabbage, garlic, leeks, spinach, berries, and nuts were some of the things used to make pottage. Kings and lords had a much richer diet that included meat and fish. Feasts given by kings and lords for special occasions could include a spectacular variety of foods.

This small painting from a medieval manuscript shows a member of the French royal family, accompanied by members of his court, arriving at one of his castles.

IS nathodex

A Feast Fit for a King

In 1397, an English lord gave a banquet for King Richard II. The menu, which still survives, included so many dishes that we can't list them all here. Among the meats were **venison** with a dish of boiled wheat, boars' heads, pork, swans, herons, pheasants, rabbits, peacocks, cranes, quails, and larks. There were also fish, such as pike and perch.

Other items on the menu were peas, a rice dish, tarts, **fritters**, broth, spiced pudding of pork, and dried fruits and eggs in a sauce of almond milk. There were also dishes called subtleties. A subtlety was a dish designed to look like something other than cooked food. For example, the feathers might be stuck back onto a roasted swan so that it looked like a living bird! The more subtleties a banquet included, the more impressive it was to guests. King Richard II's banquet included 5 subtleties.

Recipes for many dishes served at medieval feasts still survive. They often combine foods, herbs, and spices in ways that seem surprising to people today. Sampling them is one way to learn about life in the Middle Ages. Let's look at some actual medieval recipes.

This painting shows a meal being served to a king. Notice the fancy china dishes on the table. The painting comes from a manuscript titled *The Book of Good Manners*, which explained the correct way to live a good life.

Lombardy Custard

Lombardy custard was served at a feast for King Richard II on September 23, 1387. It combines dried fruits with bone **marrow** in a rich egg custard. Bone marrow adds a delicate flavor and is also rich in **nutrients**.

Lombardy custard is a fancier dish than it might first appear. Many of the items in it came from far away and were very costly during the Middle Ages. Dates and figs were imported from the Middle East. Cinnamon and a spice called mace were imported from Asia. Oranges were imported from the Mediterranean area or from the Middle East.

This picture from a map made in the late 1300s shows European traders crossing Asia to bring spices and other costly items back to Europe. The journey crossed the vast continent of Asia and took many months.

cinnamon

dried orange peel

figs

dates

You Will Need:
1 9-inch uncooked piecrust

$\frac{2}{3}$ cup prunes, cut into small pieces

$\frac{2}{3}$ cup dates, cut into small pieces

$\frac{2}{3}$ cups dried figs, cut into small pieces

2 tablespoons raw bone marrow, crumbled*

3 tablespoons fresh parsley, minced

1 cup heavy cream

2 tablespoons honey

2 eggs, lightly beaten

pinch salt

$\frac{3}{4}$ teaspoon dried orange peel

1 teaspoon cinnamon

pinch mace

* Usually you can buy soup bones at the grocery store or butcher shop and scrape the marrow out.

How to Do It:
Preheat the oven to 425°F. Prick the piecrust with a fork, then bake it for 10 minutes. Remove it from the oven and let it cool. Reduce the oven temperature to 375°F. Cover the piecrust with the prunes, dates, and dried figs. Sprinkle the bone marrow and minced parsley over the fruit. Combine all the remaining ingredients in a bowl and blend thoroughly. Pour the mixture over the fruit in the piecrust. Bake at 375°F for about 20 to 25 minutes, or until the custard is set and the top is brown. Remove from the oven and let cool for about 5 minutes before serving. Serves 8.

The recipe for Lombardy custard only serves 8 people. Imagine that you're a medieval lord hosting a feast for 16 people, which is 2 times as many. How much of the ingredients will be needed to make enough Lombardy custard for 16 people? Multiply each amount in the original recipe by 2. That's easy to do for the whole numbers. Let's look at how to handle the fractions. Let's start with $\frac{2}{3}$. The recipe calls for $\frac{2}{3}$ cup each of prunes, dates, and dried figs.

To multiply $\frac{2}{3}$ by 2, both numbers need to be fractions. Treat 2 as a fraction by placing it over the denominator 1. Multiply the numerators, then multiply the denominators. Place the product of the numerators over the product of the denominators, and you have your answer.

$$\frac{2}{1} \times \frac{2}{3} = \frac{4}{3}$$

You can't stop here, however, because $\frac{4}{3}$ is an **improper fraction**. You need to change the improper fraction to a **mixed number**. To do that, divide the numerator by the denominator. This will give you a quotient with a remainder. To complete the mixed number, place the remainder over the divisor.

$$3\overline{)4} \quad \begin{array}{r} 1 \\ \hline 4 \\ -3 \\ \hline 1 \end{array}$$

$\frac{4}{3}$ cups = $1\frac{1}{3}$ cups

To make Lombardy custard for 16 people, you'll need to use $1\frac{1}{3}$ cups each of prunes, dates, and dried figs.

The recipe also calls for $\frac{3}{4}$ teaspoon dried orange peel. To multiply $\frac{3}{4}$ by 2, go through the same steps you did for $\frac{2}{3}$.

$$\frac{2}{1} \times \frac{3}{4} = \frac{6}{4} \text{ teaspoons} \qquad \begin{array}{r} 1 \\ 4{\overline{\smash{)}6}} \\ -4 \\ \hline 2 \end{array} \qquad \frac{6}{4} = 1\frac{2}{4} \text{ teaspoons}$$

You need to perform an additional step. You need to simplify, or reduce, $\frac{2}{4}$. To do that, divide both the numerator and the denominator by the greatest common factor, which is 2. That lets you simplify $\frac{2}{4}$ to $\frac{1}{2}$.

$$1\frac{2}{4} \text{ teaspoons} = 1\frac{1}{2} \text{ teaspoons}$$

You'll need to use $1\frac{1}{2}$ teaspoons of dried orange peel.

Here, then, are the ingredients needed for enough Lombardy custard to serve 16:

1 9-inch uncooked piecrust	x 2	=	2 9-inch uncooked piecrusts
$\frac{2}{3}$ cup prunes	x 2	=	$1\frac{1}{3}$ cups prunes
$\frac{2}{3}$ cup dates	x 2	=	$1\frac{1}{3}$ cups dates
$\frac{2}{3}$ cup dried figs	x 2	=	$1\frac{1}{3}$ cups dried figs
2 tablespoons bone marrow	x 2	=	4 tablespoons bone marrow
3 tablespoons parsley	x 2	=	6 tablespoons parsley
1 cup heavy cream	x 2	=	2 cups heavy cream
2 tablespoons honey	x 2	=	4 tablespoons honey
2 eggs	x 2	=	4 eggs
pinch salt	x 2	=	2 pinches salt
$\frac{3}{4}$ teaspoon dried orange peel	x 2	=	$1\frac{1}{2}$ teapoons dried orange peel
1 teaspoon cinnamon	x 2	=	2 teaspoons cinnamon
pinch mace	x 2	=	2 pinches mace

"Golden Apples"

"Golden apples" aren't apples at all. They are pork meatballs that have been endored, or covered with a golden paste. Endoring was a popular practice at medieval feasts. Medieval cooks applied endoring paste not only to pork meatballs but to any kind of fowl. Endoring created a spectacular dish that was sure to impress guests. Sometimes medieval cooks created an even more spectacular dish by applying not just gold-colored paste but real gold to meats. The gold was applied in thin layers and was actually eaten by the guests!

The spices for "golden apples" were imported just as the spices for the Lombardy custard were. Even pepper was an imported spice!

A medieval lord might have served a feast in a dining room similar to this one.

You Will Need:

2 pounds ground pork

$\frac{3}{4}$ pound spicy pork sausage

$1\frac{1}{2}$ teaspoons salt

$1\frac{1}{2}$ teaspoons nutmeg

$1\frac{1}{2}$ teaspoons ground cloves

$\frac{3}{4}$ teaspoon ground pepper

3 eggs

$1\frac{1}{2}$ cups raisins

9 egg yolks

$\frac{3}{8}$ teaspoon turmeric

3 tablespoons flour

9 tablespoons honey

How to Do It:

Preheat the oven to 350°F. In a large bowl, combine the pork, sausage, salt, nutmeg, cloves, pepper, eggs, and raisins. Shape the pork mixture into 36 meatballs about 1 inch in diameter. Place the meatballs in a shallow pan. Bake for 20 to 25 minutes. Remove meatballs from the oven, place the pan on a wire rack, and cool. Put pan with meatballs in refrigerator for at least 30 minutes. While meatballs are in refrigerator, prepare endoring paste. Combine egg yolks, turmeric, and flour. The paste should be thick but not dry. Remove meatballs from refrigerator. Dip meatballs in endoring paste or use a pastry brush to paint paste on meatballs. Bake meatballs again at 350°F for about 15 minutes. Drip honey over meatballs and serve. Serves 12.

The recipe for "golden apples" serves 12. Imagine that you're a medieval lord who receives an unexpected visit from another lord. You must, of course, serve a feast in his honor, but there won't be a large number of guests. In fact, you'll only be serving 4 people. How much of the ingredients are needed to make "golden apples" for 4 people? The first step is to write 4 people as a fractional amount of 12 people. Four people out of 12 people can be expressed as $\frac{4}{12}$, which can be reduced to $\frac{1}{3}$. Since 4 is $\frac{1}{3}$ of 12, you'll need $\frac{1}{3}$ the amount of the ingredients in the original recipe. Remember to convert the mixed numbers in the recipe to improper fractions before you multiply by $\frac{1}{3}$.

To convert a mixed number to an improper fraction, multiply the **integer** by the denominator of the fraction. Then add the product to the numerator of the fraction to get the numerator of the improper fraction.

$$1\frac{1}{2} = \frac{(1 \times 2) + 1}{2} = \frac{3}{2}$$

Now let's calculate how much of the ingredients are needed to serve 4 people.

2 pounds ground pork	$\times \frac{1}{3} =$	$\frac{2}{3}$ pound ground pork
$\frac{3}{4}$ pound spicy pork sausage	$\times \frac{1}{3} = \frac{3}{12} =$	$\frac{1}{4}$ pound spicy pork sausage
$\frac{3}{2}$ teaspoons salt	$\times \frac{1}{3} = \frac{3}{6} =$	$\frac{1}{2}$ teaspoon salt
$\frac{3}{2}$ teaspoons nutmeg	$\times \frac{1}{3} = \frac{3}{6} =$	$\frac{1}{2}$ teaspoon nutmeg
$\frac{3}{2}$ teaspoons ground cloves	$\times \frac{1}{3} = \frac{3}{6} =$	$\frac{1}{2}$ teaspoon ground cloves
$\frac{3}{4}$ teaspoon ground pepper	$\times \frac{1}{3} = \frac{3}{12} =$	$\frac{1}{4}$ teaspoon ground pepper
3 eggs	$\times \frac{1}{3} = \frac{3}{3} =$	1 egg
$\frac{3}{2}$ cups raisins	$\times \frac{1}{3} = \frac{3}{6} =$	$\frac{1}{2}$ cup raisins
9 egg yolks	$\times \frac{1}{3} = \frac{9}{3} =$	3 egg yolks
$\frac{3}{8}$ teaspoon turmeric	$\times \frac{1}{3} = \frac{3}{24} =$	$\frac{1}{8}$ teaspoon turmeric
3 tablespoons flour	$\times \frac{1}{3} = \frac{3}{3} =$	1 tablespoon flour
9 tablespoons honey	$\times \frac{1}{3} = \frac{9}{3} =$	3 tablespoons honey

Notice that for all but 1 of the ingredients you had to perform an extra step after you multiplied the amount by $\frac{1}{3}$. You either had to reduce the fraction you got as an answer, or you had to convert an improper fraction to a whole number. There's another way to approach multiplying fractions that is often easier. You can "cancel" before you do the multiplication.

Canceling is dividing 1 factor of the numerator and 1 factor of the denominator by the same number. Canceling achieves the same results as reducing fractions. Let's see how this would work with some of the quantities from the recipe.

$$\frac{\overset{1}{\cancel{3}}}{4} \times \frac{1}{\underset{1}{\cancel{3}}} = \frac{1}{4} \times \frac{1}{1} = \frac{1}{4} \qquad \frac{\overset{1}{\cancel{3}}}{2} \times \frac{1}{\underset{1}{\cancel{3}}} = \frac{1}{2} \times \frac{1}{1} = \frac{1}{2}$$

Can you multiply $\frac{3}{8}$ by $\frac{1}{3}$ using canceling?

Makerouns

In the Middle Ages, people believed that cheese aided digestion, so they often included it in their meals. Medieval cheeses included Brie, Camembert, cheddar, cottage, farmer's, Gorgonzola, mozzarella, ricotta, Romano, Roquefort, and Stilton. The simple cheese dish known as makerouns was a favorite of the period. It combines noodles and cheese and was probably an early form of today's macaroni and cheese. Makerouns could have been made with any of the medieval hard cheeses—cheddar, Gorgonzola, mozzarella, Romano, Roquefort, or Stilton.

You Will Need:
1 pound dried egg noodles
1 tablespoon oil
$\frac{1}{8}$ teaspoon salt
2 cups grated cheese
$\frac{1}{4}$ pound butter, melted

How to Do It:
Place the noodles, oil, and salt in a large pot of boiling water. Boil for 10 to 12 minutes until the noodles are tender but still slightly firm. Drain well. Cover the bottom of a serving dish with some melted butter and grated cheese. Place a layer of noodles on top. Continue adding layers of butter, cheese, and noodles until they are used up. The top layer should be cheese. Serve immediately, or place in a 350°F oven for a few minutes and then serve. Serves 8.

Suppose you wanted to serve makerouns to 20 people. How much of the ingredients would you need? First, let's divide 20 by 8, the number of people the original recipe serves. This gives us the improper fraction $\frac{20}{8}$. We can reduce $\frac{20}{8}$ to the mixed number $2\frac{2}{4}$, then reduce that again to $2\frac{1}{2}$. Twenty is $2\frac{1}{2}$ times 8, so you would need to multiply each of the ingredients by $2\frac{1}{2}$.

Remember that when multiplication involves a mixed number, the first step is to convert the mixed number to an improper fraction. Convert the mixed number $2\frac{1}{2}$ to the improper fraction $\frac{5}{2}$.

1 pound dried egg noodles	$\times \frac{5}{2} = \frac{5}{2} =$	$2\frac{1}{2}$ pounds dried egg noodles
1 tablespoon oil	$\times \frac{5}{2} = \frac{5}{2} =$	$2\frac{1}{2}$ tablespoons oil
$\frac{1}{8}$ teaspoons salt	$\times \frac{5}{2} =$	$\frac{5}{16}$ teaspoon salt
2 cups grated cheese	$\times \frac{5}{2} = \frac{10}{2} =$	5 cups grated cheese
$\frac{1}{4}$ pound butter, melted	$\times \frac{5}{2} =$	$\frac{5}{8}$ pound butter, melted

According to legend, King Henry II declared cheddar to be the best cheese in England. His account books show that he purchased 10,240 pounds (4,649 kg) of cheddar in 1170!

Mushrooms and Leeks

Both mushrooms and leeks were eaten by rich and poor alike during the Middle Ages. Then, as now, people knew that wild mushrooms must be gathered carefully. Some are **edible**, while others are poisonous. Leeks, which are related to onions and garlic, were grown in virtually every medieval garden. They were hardy, easy to grow, and highly valued for their strong flavor. Leeks, in fact, had many uses in medieval society. They were used to treat colds and "fevers of the head." Leek juice and seeds were used in toothpaste. Leeks were even used to bleach hair!

Leeks were used in all kinds of medieval recipes. This recipe comes from the cooks of King Richard II.

Medieval kitchen gardens looked much like this historical garden at Plimouth Plantation Museum in Plymouth, Massachusetts.

You Will Need:

12 leeks

9 tablespoons butter

4 $\frac{1}{2}$ pounds mushrooms, quartered

3 cups vegetable broth

1 $\frac{1}{2}$ teaspoons honey

1 $\frac{1}{2}$ teaspoons ground ginger

9 tablespoons melted butter mixed with
   9 tablespoons flour

salt

pepper

How to Do It:

Wash the leeks carefully. Cut off and discard the roots and the green tops. Slice the leeks. Melt the butter in a very large heavy skillet or Dutch oven over medium heat. **Sauté** the leeks in the butter until they begin to wilt. Add the mushrooms and stir until they are coated with butter. In a bowl, combine the broth, honey, and ginger. Pour the liquid over the leeks and mushrooms. Cover the pan and simmer for about 5 minutes. Add the butter mixed with flour, stirring rapidly until the mixture thickens. Add salt and pepper to taste. Serves 12.

What if you want to serve mushrooms and leeks to only 8 people? How much of the ingredients would you need? The first step is to write 8 people as a fractional amount of 12 people. Eight people out of 12 people can be expressed as the fraction $\frac{8}{12}$, which can be reduced to $\frac{2}{3}$. Since 8 is $\frac{2}{3}$ of 12, you'll need $\frac{2}{3}$ the amount of the ingredients in the original recipe. Convert mixed numbers to improper fractions where necessary.

12 leeks	x $\frac{2}{3}$ = $\frac{24}{3}$ = 8 leeks
9 tablespoons butter	x $\frac{2}{3}$ = $\frac{18}{3}$ = 6 tablespoons butter
$4\frac{1}{2}$ pounds mushrooms =	
$\frac{9}{2}$ pounds mushrooms	x $\frac{2}{3}$ = $\frac{18}{6}$ = 3 pounds mushrooms
3 cups vegetable broth	x $\frac{2}{3}$ = $\frac{6}{3}$ = 2 cups vegetable broth
$1\frac{1}{2}$ teaspoons honey =	
$\frac{3}{2}$ teaspoons honey	x $\frac{2}{3}$ = $\frac{6}{6}$ = 1 teaspoon honey
$1\frac{1}{2}$ teaspoons ground ginger =	
$\frac{3}{2}$ teaspoons ground ginger	x $\frac{2}{3}$ = $\frac{6}{6}$ = 1 teaspoon ground ginger
9 tablespoons melted butter	x $\frac{2}{3}$ = $\frac{18}{3}$ = 6 tablespoons melted butter
9 tablespoons flour	x $\frac{2}{3}$ = $\frac{18}{3}$ = 6 tablespoons flour

Leeks were so highly valued during the Middle Ages that poems were written praising them.

How much of the ingredients would you need if you wanted to serve 18 people? First, let's divide 18 by 12, the number of people the original recipe serves. This gives us the fraction $\frac{18}{12}$. We can reduce $\frac{18}{12}$ to the mixed number $1\frac{6}{12}$, then reduce that again to $1\frac{1}{2}$. Since 18 is $1\frac{1}{2}$ times 12, you would need to multiply each of the ingredients by $1\frac{1}{2}$. Remember to convert this mixed number to an improper fraction before multiplying.

12 leeks	$\times \frac{3}{2} = \frac{36}{2} =$	18 leeks
9 tablespoons butter	$\times \frac{3}{2} = \frac{27}{2} =$	$13\frac{1}{2}$ tablespoons butter
$\frac{9}{2}$ pounds mushrooms	$\times \frac{3}{2} = \frac{27}{4} =$	$6\frac{3}{4}$ pounds mushrooms
3 cups vegetable broth	$\times \frac{3}{2} = \frac{9}{2} =$	$4\frac{1}{2}$ cups vegetable broth
$\frac{3}{2}$ teaspoons honey	$\times \frac{3}{2} = \frac{9}{4} =$	$2\frac{1}{4}$ teaspoons honey
$\frac{3}{2}$ teaspoons ground ginger	$\times \frac{3}{2} = \frac{9}{4} =$	$2\frac{1}{4}$ teaspoons ground ginger
9 tablespoons melted butter	$\times \frac{3}{2} = \frac{27}{2} =$	$13\frac{1}{2}$ tablespoons melted butter
9 tablespoons flour	$\times \frac{3}{2} = \frac{27}{2} =$	$13\frac{1}{2}$ tablespoons flour

Tart of Fried Fruit Slices

Tart of fried fruit slices combines apples and pears with dried fruits. Most dried fruits were imported, as were the spices. However, apples and pears were widely grown in medieval orchards. Apples and pears were, in fact, the most popular medieval fruits. Both were widely used in cooking. Prior to cooking, they underwent preparation that gave them a stronger flavor. They were either sliced and dried in the sun, sealed in clay jars that were then buried underground, or preserved in honey or **brine**.

This picture from a manuscript made in the 1400s shows apples being harvested in an orchard.

You Will Need:

1 9-inch deep-dish piecrust

3 tablespoons butter

$2\frac{1}{2}$ cups peeled, cored, and
thinly sliced apples

$2\frac{1}{2}$ cups peeled, cored, and
thinly sliced pears

$\frac{1}{2}$ cup raisins

$\frac{1}{4}$ cup pitted prunes

$\frac{1}{4}$ cup date halves

$\frac{1}{2}$ cup almond milk ($\frac{1}{2}$ cup milk with
$\frac{1}{4}$ teaspoon almond flavoring)

$\frac{1}{4}$ teaspoon cinnamon

$\frac{1}{4}$ teaspoon ground cloves

$\frac{1}{4}$ teaspoon mace

$\frac{1}{2}$ teaspoon crushed aniseed

$\frac{1}{8}$ teaspoon nutmeg

$\frac{1}{8}$ teaspoon salt

How to Do It:

Preheat the oven to 425°F. Prick the piecrust with a fork, then bake it for 10 minutes. Remove from the oven and cool on a wire rack. Reduce the oven temperature to 350°F. Melt the butter in a heavy skillet. Add the apple and pear slices. Stir and fry for about 10 minutes. Stir in the raisins, prunes, and dates. Add the almond milk, spices, and salt. Pour the mixture into the piecrust. Bake the tart at 350°F for about 40 minutes or until the

Recipes such as this were likely to be varied according to the ingredients that were available. Imagine that you're the cook for a medieval lord who wants to serve this tart at a feast, but you have only apples and no pears. If you replace the pears in the recipe with apples, how many cups of apples will you need altogether?

When adding mixed numbers, add the integers and fractions separately. Then add those sums to get the total.

$$2\frac{1}{2} \text{ cups}$$
$$+\ 2\frac{1}{2} \text{ cups}$$
$$\overline{\qquad\qquad}$$
$$4\frac{2}{2} \text{ cups} = 4 + 1 \text{ cups} = 5 \text{ cups}$$

Imagine that the only dried fruits you have are raisins. If you substitute raisins for the prunes and dates, what will be the total amount of raisins you need?

When adding fractions with different denominators, find the least common denominator of the fractions. Rename the fractions to have the least common denominator. Add the numerators, then reduce the fraction.

The recipe calls for $\frac{1}{2}$ cup raisins, $\frac{1}{4}$ cup prunes, and $\frac{1}{4}$ cup dates. The least common denominator is 4. Rename $\frac{1}{2}$ to $\frac{2}{4}$, and add the fractions. Reduce the sum.

$$\frac{2}{4} \text{ cups raisins} + \frac{1}{4} \text{ cup } \underset{\text{raisins}}{\cancel{\text{prunes}}} + \frac{1}{4} \text{ cup } \underset{\text{raisins}}{\cancel{\text{dates}}} = \frac{4}{4} = 1 \text{ cup raisins}$$

You would need 1 cup of raisins.

Now imagine that you have cinnamon and nutmeg but no cloves or mace. You decide to substitute cinnamon for the cloves and nutmeg for the mace. How much cinnamon and nutmeg will you need altogether?

The recipe calls for $\frac{1}{4}$ teaspoon cinnamon, $\frac{1}{4}$ teaspoon cloves, $\frac{1}{4}$ teaspoon mace, and $\frac{1}{8}$ teaspoon nutmeg.

$$\begin{array}{r} \frac{1}{4} \\ + \frac{1}{4} \\ \hline \frac{2}{4} = \frac{1}{2} \end{array}$$

You will need $\frac{1}{2}$ teaspoon cinnamon.

$$\begin{array}{r} \frac{1}{4} \\ + \frac{1}{8} \\ \hline \end{array} = \begin{array}{r} \frac{2}{8} \\ + \frac{1}{8} \\ \hline \frac{3}{8} \end{array}$$

You will need $\frac{3}{8}$ teaspoon nutmeg.

Now look back at the recipe on page 25, which serves 8 people. How much of the ingredients would you need if you wanted to serve 16 people?

Nutmeg comes from nuts of the nutmeg tree. Mace comes from the bright red covering on the nuts.

Sambocade

Medieval feasts commonly included a dessert. Sambocade, an early form of the modern cheesecake, provided another opportunity to include cheese in the feast. It is flavored with the addition of dried elderflowers and rosewater. Flowers had many practical uses in medieval society, and roses in particular were used in a wide variety of ways. They were used as a fragrance for women and houses, as medicine, and as flavoring in many sweet foods.

You Will Need:

1 9-inch piecrust
$1\frac{1}{2}$ pounds cottage cheese
$\frac{1}{3}$ cup honey
3 egg whites
2 tablespoons dried elderflowers
1 tablespoon rosewater

How to Do It:

Preheat the oven to 350°F. Combine the cottage cheese, honey, egg whites, elderflowers, and rosewater. Blend thoroughly. Pour mixture into the piecrust. Bake for about 1 hour, or until the filling has set and the piecrust is golden brown. Don't worry if the filling still jiggles a little. It will finish setting as it cools. Remove from the oven, cool, and serve. Serves 8.

Imagine that you're the cook for a medieval lord. You have both cottage cheese and ricotta cheese on hand and decide to use a combination of both in this recipe. If you use equal amounts of each kind of cheese, how much of each will you need?

To divide a fraction by an integer, treat the integer as a fraction and place it over the denominator 1. Invert the divisor, then multiply the fractions.

The integer in this case is 2, which is $\frac{2}{1}$ when written as a fraction. Invert it to get $\frac{1}{2}$, then multiply $\frac{3}{2}$ by $\frac{1}{2}$.

$$\frac{3}{2} \div \frac{2}{1} = \frac{3}{2} \times \frac{1}{2} = \frac{3}{4}$$

You will need $\frac{3}{4}$ pound of cottage cheese and $\frac{3}{4}$ pound of ricotta cheese.

Elderflowers are the tiny white flowers of the elder tree or shrub. They turn brown when they are dried. Elderflowers were used to flavor food and drinks and as medicine.

How the Medieval Taste for Spices Changed the World

Imported spices were a great expense for the kings and lords who could afford to enjoy them in their food. They were a source of wealth for the merchants and traders who supplied them to kings and lords. In the late Middle Ages, driven by dreams of great riches, many Europeans set out to find new trade routes to the Asian sources of the sought-after spices. They were especially seeking sea routes that would be faster and less dangerous than the known land routes. At first, they looked for ways around Africa. However, the continent proved to be much larger than the early European explorers had realized.

Then, in the late 1400s, Christopher Columbus decided to reach the East by sailing west across the Atlantic Ocean. Like other Europeans, Columbus was unaware of the existence of North and South America. He and others believed that Asia lay on the other side of the Atlantic. In 1492, after the Spanish monarchs agreed to finance his expedition, Columbus set sail. He did not find the spices he was seeking. Instead, he found a "New World," forever changing the course of history.

Glossary

brine (BRYN) A solution of water and salt.

edible (EH-duh-buhl) Fit to be eaten.

feudal (FYOO-duhl) Having to do with the social system of medieval Europe in which the king occupied the top level, with lords below him and serfs below lords.

fritter (FRIH-tuhr) A small mass of fried batter with some kind of filling, such as fruit, meat, or cheese.

improper fraction (im-PRAH-puhr FRAK-shun) A fraction in which the numerator is equal to or larger than the denominator.

integer (IN-tih-juhr) A positive or negative whole number.

marrow (MEHR-oh) A kind of tissue that is found inside bones.

mixed number (MIKST NUHM-buhr) A number made up of an integer and a fraction.

nutrient (NOO-tree-uhnt) Something that contributes to growth and provides energy.

pinch (PINCH) A tiny amount that can be held between the thumb and finger.

Renaissance (reh-nuh-SAHNS) The period of a rebirth of classical learning that followed the Middle Ages in Europe. In some places, it began in the early 1300s. It lasted until the late 1500s.

sauté (saw-TAY) To fry in a small amount of fat, such as butter or oil.

venison (VEH-nuh-suhn) The flesh of a deer.

Index